Rock Climbing

Published by Creative Education

P.O. Box 227, Mankato, Minnesota 56002

Creative Education is an imprint of The Creative Company

Design and production by Blue Design, Portland, Maine

Printed in the United States of America

Photographs by Getty Images (Iconica, National Geographic,

Photographer's Choice, Photonica, Taxi)

Library of Congress Cataloging-in-Publication Data

Fandel, Jennifer.

Rock climbing / by Jennifer Fandel.

p. cm. — (Active sports)

Includes index.

ISBN-13: 978-1-58341-468-2

1. Rock climbing—Juvenile literature. I. Title.

GV200.2.F36 2007

796.52'23—dc22   2006018703

First Edition

9 8 7 6 5 4 3 2 1

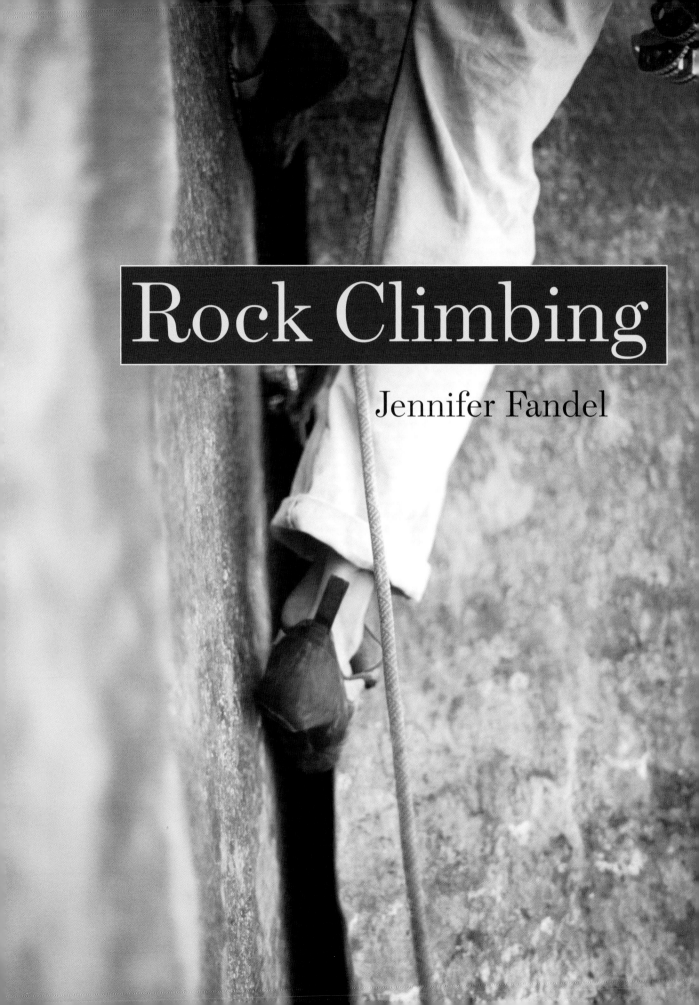

Rock Climbing

Jennifer Fandel

This is a famous rock calléd El Capitan.

You feel hard rock under your feet. You grab a piece of rock. You look down. It is a long way to the ground. Rock climbing can be scary!

Lots of people climb in the Rocky Mountains.

Rock climbers climb tall rocks.
The rocks reach straight up
toward the sky. Some of the rocks
are smooth. Others are rough.
There is snow on some rocks.

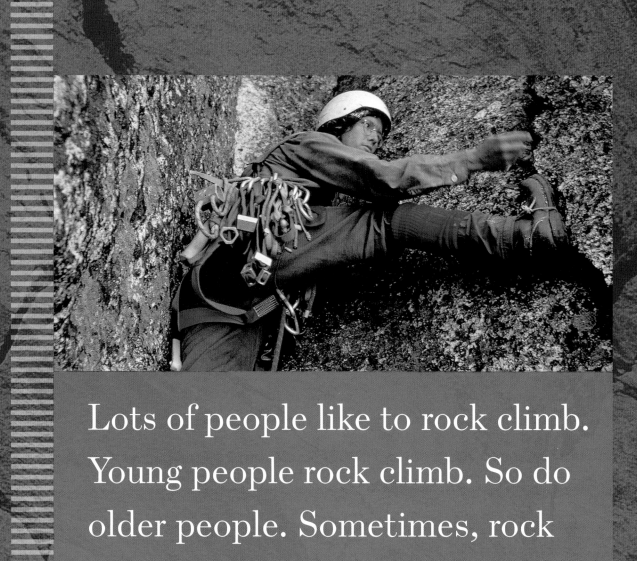

Lots of people like to rock climb. Young people rock climb. So do older people. Sometimes, rock climbers try to climb the same rock many times. Some people never get to the top. They keep trying, though!

Some climbers go up very tall rocks.

Rock climbing is hard work. Rock climbers must be strong. They have to be **flexible**, too. To rock climb, climbers reach above their head. They grab bumps on the rock with their hands. They find cracks in the rock. This is where they put their feet.

In snowy places, rock climbers wear special boots.

Climbing rocks can be **dangerous**. Climbers wear a helmet to **protect** their head. Helmets keep climbers safe from falling rocks. Helmets protect climbers' heads if they fall, too.

Wearing a helmet is important in rock climbing.

Most climbers use a rope to keep them safe. They tie one end of the rope to themselves. They can tie the other end to a rock. Or they can tie it to a climbing **partner**. If a climber slips, the rope catches him or her.

Special ropes are used to keep climbers safe.

Climbing a big rock can take all day.

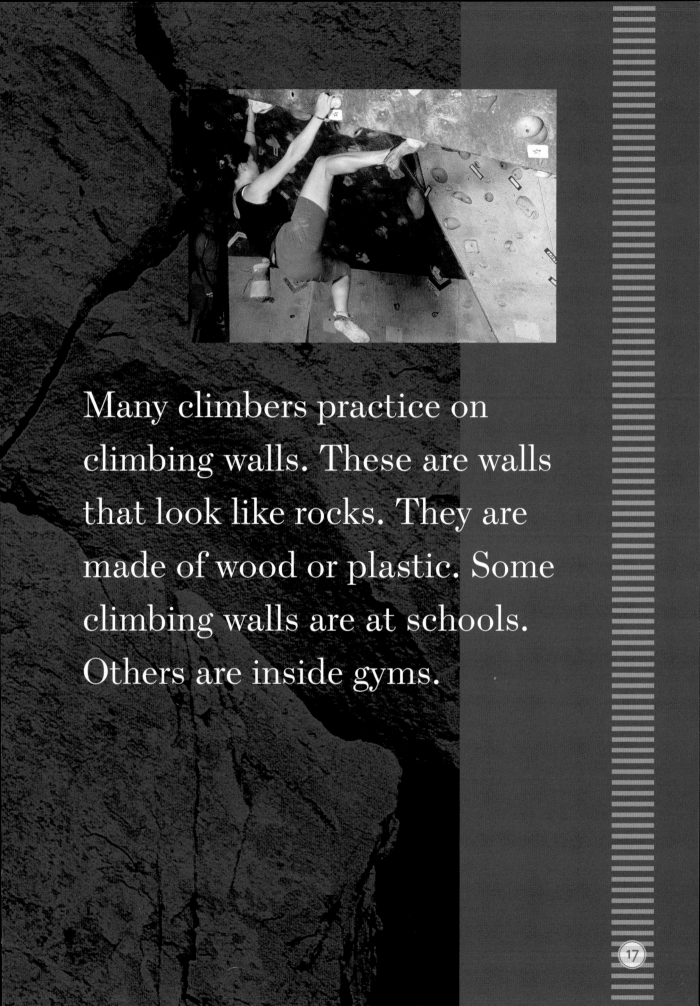

Many climbers practice on climbing walls. These are walls that look like rocks. They are made of wood or plastic. Some climbing walls are at schools. Others are inside gyms.

Most people climb rocks with a partner.

Lots of climbers take lessons. Climbing teachers show people how to climb. Lots of people try to climb climbing walls first. Then they try to climb small rocks. One day, they might try to climb big rocks!

Climbing rocks is a good way to become strong.

New rock climbers stay close to the ground.

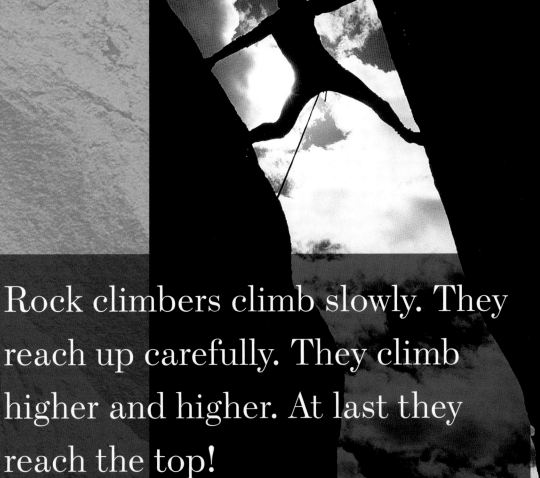

Rock climbers climb slowly. They reach up carefully. They climb higher and higher. At last they reach the top!

GLOSSARY

dangerous—not safe

flexible—able to bend easily

partner—a person you do things with

protect—keep safe

INDEX